Landmark Vi

Visiting We

Anglesey

Bardsey Island

Lindsey Porter

Published by
The Horizon Press

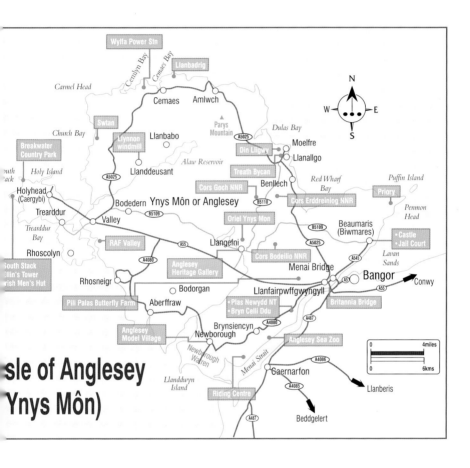

Isle of Anglesey
(Ynys Môn)

Published in the UK by:
Horizon Editions Ltd
Trading as The Horizon Press,
The Oaks, Moor Farm Road West, Ashbourne, Derbyshire DE6 1HD
e-mail books@thehorizonpress.co.uk

1st Edition

ISBN 978-1-84306-503-6

© **Lindsey Porter 2010**

Printed by: Gomer Press Limited, Llandysul, Ceredigion, Wales
Cartography and Design: Mark Titterton

Picture Credits:

Page 2: Newborough Forest
Front cover: Britannia Bridge. **Back Cover top:** South Stack Lighthouse, Holyhead
bottom: Llanddwyn Island; **bottom right:** Bardsey Mountain, Bardsey Island

Anglesey Sea Zoo: p18

Colin Macdonald: p54 top

Ben Porter: 59 (both), 63 (both), back cover bottom right

All other photography by the author

Acknowledgements

I wish to acknowledge the assistance I have received from Helen Maurice Jones in many aspects of the production of this book and for suggesting it in the first place. Also to the Porter family on Bardsey; Joanna (Helen's sister), Steve, Rachel and Ben (who took the photographs I have used here). It is coincidence that we share the same surname. Also to Anglesey Sea Zoo for the images they provided.

DISCLAIMER

While every care has been taken to ensure that the information in this guide is as accurate as possible at the time of publication, the publisher and author accept no responsibility for any loss, injury or inconvenience sustained by anyone using this book. Please note that some attractions may open differently and that times may vary. Maps are for info only, please use a road map.

Contents

Top Tips

Plas Newydd (NT): home of the Marquis of Anglesey by Menai Strait

Menai Bridges: memorable views of two 19th century bridges

Bryn Celli Ddu: large chambered tomb near Plas Newydd

Din Lligwi/Holyhead Roman Fort: two important sites of Roman period

Beaumaris Castle, Court and Goal: World Heritage Site castle plus former court and goal

South Stack/Ellin's Tower: for the view and bird observatory

Llanddwyn Beach: (for younger children) and Rosneigr Beach (for beach sports)

Anglesey Sea Zoo: important maritime learning centre

Oriel Ynys Mon: the island's central arts centre

Llynnon Windmill: restored windmill, shop sells Anglesey produce

Best Beaches

There are many beaches and coves around the coast. Amongst the best beaches are those at Benllech (chiefly Red Wharf Bay) and its eastwards extension, Llanddona Beach; Church Bay, north of Holyhead off the A5025 to Cemaes and Amlwch; Llanddwyn Beach at Newborough Forest and Warren with miles of soft sand either side of Llanddwyn Island; and Porth Darfarch, halfway between Trearddur and South Stack. Rhosneigr and Trearddur beaches are popular for paragliding and other beach sports. The tide recedes a good distance between high and low tide level on many beaches.

Welcome to
Anglesey/Ynys Mon

Anglesey, or Ynys Mon, lies just off the North Wales coast. In a sense it is unfortunate that Snowdonia is such a dramatic draw for visitors. Anglesey does not have high mountains, deep valleys or narrow gauge railways. Yet its coast is arguably as attractive and dramatic in places, justifying its Area of Outstanding Beauty Status on virtually the whole of the island's coastline. Who would argue that its two bridges across the Menai Strait are not iconic views of national interest, especially Telford's graceful Menai suspension bridge.

Opposite page:Menai Bridge, built in 1826. When the first chain was placed across the Strait, several workmen walked across it.

Left: The Britannia Bridge

The island has an incredible wealth of prehistoric remains dotted across the landscape. The Roman fort at Holyhead is almost like a best kept secret, its high walls still surviving largely intact. Near to Moelfre is the equally intriguing Romano-British village at Din Lligwy with nearby burial chamber, with its enormous capstone still in place.

The coastal path is a delight: combining dramatic scenery, lovely bays, sandy beaches and plenty of distractions en-route, such as the two Menai Bridges, Beaumaris Castle and Plas Newydd. With dual carriageway access all the way from the M6 to Holyhead and a main line railway, getting there is no longer the car-choked headache it used to be.

There is much to see, do and explore on Anglesey. It is ideal for a week's break with something different to do everyday. This book highlights the more interesting features, but it does not cover in any detail the coastal path, the many inns in quiet corners, or facilities for visiting boat crews.

Anglesey actually consists principally of two islands, Anglesey and Holy Island which accommodates Holyhead with its ferry facilities to Ireland. There are several smaller islands, including Puffin Island near Beaumaris, the largest of the uninhabited islands.

North Wales does have another inhabited island. It is Bardsey at the

Above: The statue of Nelson below Llanfair Parish Church

Above: The Marquis of Anglesey's Column

end of the Lleyn peninsula. It has been included together with details on how to get there.

If you are prepared to explore the back roads which characterise Anglesey, you will find the island a delight. In a sense it is almost a paradox that road access is confined to two bridges, one of 1826 and the other a new road on an 1846 railway bridge still carrying trains. At the other end of the island huge modern ferryboats carry you away to Ireland from Holyhead while high tech jets nip in and out of neighbouring RAF Valley, soaring over the Snowdonia mountains with effortless ease. Only the high chimney of the defunct aluminium works at Holyhead plus the winding gear on the metal mine on Parys Mountain (also disused at the moment) show how external economic conditions can have an impact on the economy here.

There is such a lot to see and do on Anglesey. It is an absorbing island and once hooked, it will draw you back time and time again. I hope you enjoy the experience and fun here as much as I do.

The Anglesey Coastal Path

The island is most fortunate in having a coastline which is mainly scenic and with the obvious exceptions of coastal communities, is largely undeveloped. A footpath 125 miles/200km in length has been established around the island and is becoming increasingly popular. Because of the coastal communities, there is a bus service close to the path in most areas. It is a diverse route way too, with the high cliffs in the north and north-west, plenty of lovely bays, several nature reserves, the large wooded and sand dune covered areas near Newborough and the different landscape fronting Menai Strait, with the mountain backdrop beyond.

For diversion, there are a few pre-Norman church sites (with a more modern building on the site), all however still of significant age; the Priory at Penmon Point; the large surviving walls of the Holyhead Roman fort; Beaumaris Castle; elegant Plas Newydd; water sports at Rhosneigr and Trearddur; nature reserves and even the Visitor Centre at Wylfa Nuclear Power Station plus RAF Valley.

Moreover, virtually the whole of the coastline and its hinterland is in an Area of Outstanding Natural Beauty. You do not get a much better recommendation than that to include the path (at least in part) in your visit to Anglesey.

It is shown on the modern OS Map and there is a bi-lingual book describing the route.

Anglesey/
Ynys Mon

The **Menai Strait** was a formidable barrier to trade and transport with Anglesey before Telford arrived with a solution in mind. The Act of Union with Ireland in 1801 brought increased traffic from Dublin to London and vice versa. The road to the ferry across the Strait came from Aber via the Sychnant Pass from Conwy and Penmaenmawr. It struck fear into all travellers except those with the strongest of will or maybe the strongest of ale. The road along the precipitous cliffs was only seven feet wide and had no secure barrier to prevent swinging coaches going over the sheer drop to the sea. It was also prone to rocks crashing down from above, dislodged by animals or frost.

It was so bad that the city of Dublin, in 1770, subscribed to the cost of building a wall 4.5 ft/1.37m in height. This stirred the Government to fund further improvements soon after and this lasted until Telford's new road from Conwy was built. The ferry used to leave for Porthaethwy, now **Menai Bridge**, where The George Inn provided hospitality for travellers. However, it was to be made largely redundant by Telford's bold and imaginative Menai Bridge, opened on 3rd January 1826.

This high and elegant structure was built high on Admiralty insistence so that ship's masts would be unhindered. In fact it is 100 ft/30.5m from the bridge deck to the swirling waters below at high tide. Telford suspended the bridge deck carrying the roads (one each way) from four enormous chains (each consisting of 4 chains) made up from 33,264 flat iron bars made at Upton Magna, near Shrewsbury. These were replaced in 1938-41 by two sets of stronger and lighter steel chains still made up from flat bars. This enabled the inner two sets of chains to be removed and also permitted a heavier traffic load on the bridge. Another advantage was that the removal of the vertical bars attaching the bridge deck to the two former middle chains meant that the carriageways could be widened.

The opening of the bridge was a great celebration; the first vehicle over the bridge at 1.30am was the London mail coach. With daylight, there was an uninterrupted stream of carriages, carts, horsemen and pedestrians crossing the bridge.

Near the bridge on a little island is the small church of **Llandysilio**. It is reached by a causeway. The original foundation was in 630 by St Tysilio (Llandysilio means the church of Tysilio). It was rebuilt in the early years of the 15th century.

Above: Llanfair P.G. railway station

Below: Llanfair Tollhouse

Above and below: Bryn Celli Ddu burial mound

The **Britannia Tubular Bridge** was built a couple of decades after the Menai Bridge. Originally constructed by the famous railway engineer Robert Stephenson, it was solely a railway bridge when destroyed by fire in the 1980s. It was rebuilt as a twin-deck bridge, with a road above the railway. At the western end of the bridge two large and majestic stone lions guard the entrance to the railway bridge. Today, traffic roars up and down above these unseen silent guardians of the bridge, visible from the safety of St Mary's Church car-park (see below).

There are two more lions guarding the mainland approach to the bridge. They are all of limestone and in Egyptian-style, each carved from 11 pieces of stone. They are 12ft/3.6m tall, 25ft/7.6m long and each weighs 30 tons.

The railway bridge was built in 1846-50. It followed on from the experience gained from the smaller tubular railway bridge, built at Conwy, in 1846-48. The Britannia Bridge was much longer and heavier, with strong towers to take the weight of the rectangular tubes jacked up from below. The site took advantage of a rock in the middle of the Strait, upon which was built the Britannia Tower, which stands 230 ft/70m high. The four tubes weighed c. 2,500 tons each. Such was the strength of the whole structure, it was sufficient to carry the weight of the combined rail and road bridge after the fire.

This bridge is regarded as Stephenson's bridge. However, since the reconstruction, only the stonework is his. The steelwork structure is that of RJ Coon and built in 1970-2. Mr Coon was the Chief Civil Engineer of British Railways. One supposes that it is now the Stephenson-Coon bridge, but it is unlikely that the name of one of our greatest Victorian engineers will be ousted.

Another guardian of a generation earlier maybe seen nearby and is quite unexpected. Turning off the A55 at the Anglesey end of the bridge and then almost immediately left again brings you to the car-park of **Llanfair parish church** (it is signposted to St Mary's Church).

You are immediately struck by the Britannia Bridge towering above but beyond the church is what appears to be another huge monument in the churchyard. It is in fact beyond the churchyard and is a statue to Lord Nelson, built on the foreshore. His sword has rotted away in the salt-laden air but the stonework remains. At low tide you can walk around it, but the rocks are slippery, so take extra care. On the far side is the famous message Nelson had fluttering from the rigging of HMS *Victory* prior to the Battle of Trafalgar in 1805: 'England expects every man will do his duty'.

Today, it is often not appreciated that the word 'expects' should be read as 'knows' in this morale-boosting final message from the commander to his men. They did do their duty and Wales can be proud that many of her sons stood and were counted that day.

It is worth stopping off and walking down to the monument, especially at low tide for the views along the Strait, especially towards the Britannia Bridge. **The monument** was built by Clarence Paget, son of the 1st Marquis of Anglesey in 1873, in time for the 70th anniversary of the Battle of Trafalgar. The statue records that Clarence was the sculptor too, although one assumes he designed it rather than carved the stone. Looking down the Strait (south), you will see **Plas Newydd** on the Anglesey bank (see below).

Proceeding on the old, Telford-built road towards Holyhead, one soon comes to **Llanfair P.G.** where one of three remaining former toll houses on the road may be seen. Unusually, the painted list of tolls chargeable when the gates were thrown open remains intact. The road was mainly built by 1822 and this was the last surviving toll house in Wales (1895). To the right, rising above the trees nearby and north of the A5, is a monument to the 1st Marquis of Anglesey, one of the Paget family. They gave up their seat at Beaudesert on Cannock Chase south of Stafford to live on their other estate adjacent to the Strait – Plas Newydd. This is now open to the public and is nearby on the A4080 to Newborough (see below).

The monument is a **tall stone column** of 1816, with steps inside to give access to a viewing platform at the top. The Marquis lost a leg to a cannon ball at the Battle of Waterloo in 1815. He was the cavalry commander as Lord Paget. The statue was added later in 1860 after his death. Lord Paget said to the Duke of Wellington 'my God Sir, I've lost my leg' to which came the response 'my God Sir, so you have'. His replacement wooden leg may still be seen at Plas Newydd. The monument is built upon a rare rock called blue schist.

Also at Plas Newydd is the original name board from the nearby railway station at **Llanfairpwllg-wyngyllgogerychwyrndrobwll-llantysiliogogogoch** – the longest place name in the world. It means St Mary's Church in a hollow by the white hazel close to the rapid whirlpool by the red cave of St Tysilio. Today the name is reduced to the more manageable Llanfair P.G., although of course it is used in full for the benefit of the tourist trade. The railway station which uses its full name is still open and there is a large shopping outlet adjacent (Pringles). Llanfair P.G. holds the distinction of having the first branch in Britain of the Women's Institue (1915). The **W.I. room** is next to the toll house.

Above: Llanfair P.G., Women's Institute

Below: Newborough Forest

Taking the A4080 towards Newborough, in 1.5 miles/2.4km, a sign to the left leads into the National Trust car-park for Plas Newydd. This is a lovely 18th century house and no trip to Anglesey would be complete without visiting here. The home of the Marquis of Anglesey, it passed to the National Trust in 1976. The garden is extensive, with memorable views up the adjacent Menai Strait to the Britannia Bridge.

Rex Whistler came to stay and whilst here, painted in the dining room a wonderful scene of a Mediterranean harbour. His mural fills one large wall. He portrays Romeo (a self portrait) and Juliet (portraying Caroline, daughter of the 6th Marquis, with whom he was very much in love). His genius shows through, for when you enter the room and see the painting, there are wet footprints which come towards you from the quayside. If you walk the length of this long room and look back at the painting, the footprints are still coming towards you!

So many people go back to recheck, that the room's floor covering regularly wears through. However, your eyes do not deceive you; the optical illusion is there. There is a shop and good tearoom here, but try and save enough time to visit a nearby burial mound. Don't confuse it with another in the Plas Newydd grounds.

This is no insignificant heap of earth and stone. It is near Llanddaniel and involves a short 7-minute walk by a stream. When you reach a footbridge, cross over and continue on.

It is called **Bryn Celli Ddu** (in English, say Brin Kelly Dee). It has a well preserved passageway to an 8 ft/2.4m wide inner chamber and is one of two (the other is between Aberffraw and Rhosneigr further along the A4080) which are unique in Wales, having mysterious designs inscribed on stone.

The chambered tomb was constructed in the middle of a henge monument, which consisted of a circular ditch and 14 vertical stones, built in c. 3000 BC. An adjacent sign points out that henges are unusual in Wales, but more common in England (eg. Stonehenge). This suggests that long lines of communication probably existed at that time. It is also worth remembering that Stonehenge itself includes stones taken there from the Prescilly Hills in Pembrokeshire, South Wales, emphasising the Welsh link.

To get there, turn left on leaving Plas Newydd and at the cross roads turn right for just under a mile. It is on your right and big enough to be visible across the fields. The car-park is by the village sign for **Llanddaniel**, at the side of the road.

Continuing down the A4080, **Brynsiencyn** is reached, where a lane leads down to the **Anglesey Sea Zoo**. Ideal on a wet day (as is Plas Newydd) the zoo houses examples of sea life from all around the coast of Britain, including some rare species. A little further on (2-3 miles/4-5km), the B4419 goes left down to the Strait at **Tan-y-Foel**. Here is the pier remains for the former Foel Ferry which, until 1954, took foot passengers to Caernarfon. There are good views from this quiet backwater across the Strait towards the town with the mountains of Snowdonia beyond. There is a working farm – **Foel** – here, which has developed into a tourist attraction.

Look out also for the signs to **Anglesey Model Village and Gardens**, just beyond Dwyran. They opened in 1992 and are annually extended. They're set in one acre of landscaped gardens and have a tearoom and picnic area.

Just past Dwyran is the roundabout at Pen-Iôn. Immediately before that, a path goes left down a track towards stepping stones across the Afon Braint. There are about two dozen of them, but despite being large they may be submerged by a high tide. At the roundabout, there is a left turn to a car-park with access on to **Newborough Warren** and the sand dunes.

Newborough was previously called Rhosyr, but was given a borough charter (from which its name is derived) by Edward I. In the middle of town is a minor cross roads and the left turn (signposted for the car-park) goes past the chapel (on right) and cemetery (on left) on to Newborough Forest, a 3,400 acre/1376ha parcel of land carved out of Newborough Warren and planted with pine trees to stabilise the sand dunes. You have to pay a fee to continue down to the car-park, close to the beach. There is a large nature reserve here, forest walks, dunes and miles of fine soft sand on the beach.

Here it is never crowded you just walk a little further to find your own space. It is terrific for children (of all ages!). The adjacent sea (Cardigan Bay) attracts turtles, literally from across the Atlantic, seeking the many jellyfish which are their staple diet. Sometimes the jellyfish are washed up onto the beach and should be avoided; their sting is painful and there can occasionally be lots of them.

Although the car-park has a toilet block, you need to take with you all you are likely to require, as there is no shop etc at the beach.

The dunes are chiefly grass-covered (beyond the forest to the east and west) and this is kept down by ponies, sheep and rabbits. It maintains a healthy regime of plant life and the area is one of the largest areas of sand dunes in Europe.

A rocky promontory here is **Llanddwyn Island** (though now with a neck of sand connecting it to **Newborough Forest**). The island is also part of the nature reserve and several paths enable you to see many

*Three photographs of
Anglesey Sea Zoo*

Above: Newborough Beach

Above: Llanddwyn Island

19

wildflowers and the birdlife. The former church is now a ruin. At the far end of this elongated island are the lifeboat station and lighthouse. Adjacent cottages are now used as a visitor centre. There are remarkable examples of pillow lava to be seen here. It was created by lava extruding onto the seabed in former times and cooling very quickly. Look out for it at Pilot's Cove at the far end of the island.

There is currently a plan to remove about 40 per cent of the trees and return the land to dune land. It includes the land adjacent to the coast and alters forever the lovely walk through the trees close to the beach on a forest road which gives access to trails and Llanddwyn Island. This is an important issue, not only for the red squirrels and ravens here, but equally important for visitors. The Anglesey economy depends on visitors and the contribution it makes. This forest area needs better marketing for the recreational input it can make, rather than sawn down. If you wish to see what it will look like, just walk on to the dunes to the east. The peaceful forest ambience, so important to so many, disappears completely.

Beyond Newborough is a large area known as the **Malltreath Sands**, really an extension of the Warren. Behind it is Malltreath Marsh, a low-lying area now largely drained and given over to pasture. The Sands are a **National Nature Reserve**.

Telford built his A5 over the marsh but it is the inland side of the A4080 which silted up. It formerly ran inland almost to **Llangefni** – a distance of nearly 12 miles/19km. The seaward side of the estuary remained basically as it was, grass-covered sand, plus a large area of water and a haven for wild life, now of national importance as a result. The Afon Cefni flows through it. North of the A4080 the river is in an artificial narrow channel (with excess water in the old river course adjacent) but on the seaward side it is wide and shallow.

A little distance further west is the village of **Aberffraw** on the Afon (River) Ffraw, which flows parallel to the Cefni, but is smaller. Aberffraw was the home of the Welsh Princes of Gwynedd, but their palace no longer remains. What there is here is a particularly fine sandy beach at Aberffraw Bay. The next bay to the north-west, beyond the headland of Aberffraw Bay is **Porth Cwyfan**. In the bay is a rocky outcrop with a simple church originally founded in the 7th century and dedicated to St Cwyfan. It is surrounded by a retaining wall to prevent erosion by the sea and is approached by a causeway accessible at low tide.

There are more enticing small bays on the Holyhead side, such as at **Trecastell**, 2 miles/3km further on from Aberffraw. Of national importance here, however, is not the beach but the ancient monument

Barclodiad y Gawres. This is the other chambered burial mound matching Bryn Celli Ddu (see above). It is considered to be up to 4,000 years old with inscribed patterns carved on some of the stones.

The road gives access to a rough surfaced car-park at the head of the beach. At the Rhosneigr side is a path leading to the burial mound. It is where the path turns right and descends. This mound upon being excavated revealed a circular chambered tomb – a circle of large stone and a capstone above part of it. Several of the stones were carved 2-3,000 years ago. A concrete roof protects the tomb and you could go inside to inspect the carvings. Now it is gated off because of graffiti as modern youth attempted to provide a contrast to the prehistoric designs. You can see in, but not see any of the carvings. However, the interpretation board gives details of how to gain access.

A little further is **Rhosneigr**, perhaps the nearest thing on Anglesey to a holiday resort. It is situated between two sandy bays, has an 18-hole golf course and good cliff walking on the coastal path. It is popular for water sports, paragliding etc. Its neighbour is **RAF Valley**, the regional air/sea rescue centre, established in 1941.

RAF Valley is also the home of Number 4 Flying Training School (4FTS), a recent member being Prince William. It was formed in 1960 and aircraft enthusiasts will see regular flights of Hawk aircraft plus Sea King helicopters. The station is the busiest in the whole of the RAF.

Its near neighbour, by contrast, is another connected with control of the skies – the RSPB. Its reserve consists of reed-fringed lakes, with a varied bird population including tufted ducks, pochards, shovellers, gadwalls and grebes. It is open daily (free access). Access is from Junction 4 on the A55 (signposted Bodedern and Caergeiliog). Follow MOD signs to RAF Valley. On reaching a lake on the right, continue to the end of the lake and then look for the entrance (also on the right). ☎ 01407 764973

During the construction of the runways, a huge hoard of Iron Age relics and animal bones was found, again of national importance. They are now in the National Museum, Cardiff and the collection is known as the Llyn Cerrig Bach hoard.

Across **Cwmyran Bay** from Rhosneigr is **Holy Island**, reached across the Stanley Embankment if taking the A5. Its Welsh name is Ynys Gybi, after St Cybi, who established a church here within the walls of the **Roman fort**. Its successor still exists within the tall remains of the impressive Roman walls.

With the Act of Union of 1801, Holyhead was chosen as the seaport for Dublin, with Telford constructing the A5 from London (Marble

21

Above: Aberffraw Bay

Below: Porth Cwyfan

Above: Rhosneigr

Below: Trearddur

Arch) to Holyhead. His road created a fast, well constructed road for the journey. However, Holyhead remained into the 19th century as a shabby, uncompromising place for travellers unfortunate enough to have to stay there, waiting for a boat. The A5 ended at a less elaborate '**Marble Arch**' in the Holyhead Docks. There is no public access to it at present but it can be clearly viewed from parts of the town.

Fortunately matters have changed for the better. Holyhead is a popular yachting centre with safe mooring. The ships on the ferry routes to Ireland are modern, including large and fast catamarans. Today, these ships deliver you to Ireland, Dublin and Dun Laoghaire, in only 90 minutes. For those of us not heading over the sea, heading over Holyhead Mountain is recommended, to **South Stack**. Here the lighthouse station, automated in 1984, is now a Trinity House Visitor Centre. Unfortunately the bridge to the small island of South Stack is down 400 steps! However, many people come to see the puffins, guillemots and other seabirds that nest on the cliffs, as well as the lighthouse.

Nearby, the RSPB occupies an observation tower called Ellin's Tower. It is an interpretation centre with free admission. Powerful glasses enable you to see the seabirds close up, across the inlet, at South Stack Island.

Ellin's Tower takes its name from Ellin, wife of the Anglesey M.P., William Stanley. He built it for her as an observation tower in 1867. It was becoming derelict when purchased by the RSPB in 1980. They refurbished the building and opened it in 1982. Today it is a popular attraction for ornithologists and curious passers-by alike. It is painted white as an aid to shipping.

Opposite the car-park/café above Ellin's Tower, a stile into the field brings you to a group of hut circles. They are the low walls of former settlements, thought to be houses dating from 2nd-4th century AD. They are known as the **Irishmen's Huts** and an interpretation board explains what there is to see and something of the site's history. If you take the lane from here to Trearddur, after about 1.5 miles/2.4km, look out for two Bronze Age **standing stones** which are about 10 ft/3m in height. They are near the village of Penrhosfeilw and up a lane to the left. Further down the south coast is Trearddur, popular with water sport enthusiasts. It sits on a narrow neck of land where the sea almost divides Holy Island.

There are now three roadways onto the island: via the B4545 from Valley to Trearddur; the A5 and the A55 from Valley to Holyhead. If you are heading for the ferry, the A55 delivers you quickly and without hindrance to the dock gate.

The breakwater here is 1.5 miles/2.4km in length. Much of the stone (some 7 million tons of it) came from the Breakwater Quarries nearby, the area now being a country park.

The road to the old quarries, now the **Breakwater Country Park**, begins near to the **Holyhead Maritime Museum**. The latter is worth a visit, especially for those with a curiosity for the island's maritime history. It is housed in the oldest surviving lifeboat house in Wales (c. 1858). It is an interesting looking building in itself and situated on Newry Beach, by Holyhead Harbour.

The construction of the breakwater, at the time, was probably the largest civil engineering project in the country being built. Construction started in 1845 and took until 1873 to complete. It cost £1.285m and some 1,500 men were employed on it.

At the quarries is a small visitor centre and good interpretation boards giving details on the project. The country park has way-marked trails plus an audio trail, downloadable onto an mp3 player or compatible phone from the Visit Anglesey website: www.visitanglesey.co.uk or from the Country Park Visitor Centre. A group of ten ponies keep the grass down, which in turn encourages small plants to flourish. The Country Park links up with the coastal path, which gives access to South Stack and Ellin's Tower mentioned above.

The old quarry faces (eleven of them) should be avoided as they are dangerous and under no circumstances climbed.

The shipping lane to Liverpool created a method of payment. Ships passing Holyhead to Liverpool were within a day of their destination, fair weather permitting. It became practice to advise shipping offices ahead from Holyhead that a particular vessel had been sighted.

Merchants in the port were then advised that their goods (and their payment for them) would be due the following day, payment being due under the contract 'one day after sight'. Signal towers enabled the message to be passed on to Liverpool in seconds, rather than minutes.

The shipping lanes around this coast are notoriously dangerous and shipping losses in the area attest this.

On the way to the Breakwater Country Park, the coastal road passes the **Maritime Museum**. It has a restaurant and a significant exhibition of various shipwrecks and other nautical material, including some large and very fine models of actual vessels. One large glass case displays details and artefacts relating to *HMS Thetis* (see p40) which sunk taking 99 men with her. The men are commemorated on a memorial in Holyhead cemetery and most of the 99 are buried here. The youngest was only 18 years old.

Above: Standing Stones near Penrhosfeilw

Below: Ellin's Tower, South Stack, Holyhead

South Stack Lighthouse, Holyhead

This attraction is well worth a visit, but check if open in winter.

North of Holyhead

Some 6 miles/9km north of Holyhead is a new museum at **Porth Swtan/Church Bay**. The **Swtan museum** is the last thatched cottage on Anglesey and is now restored as a heritage site. It is situated off the car-park at Church Bay. The cottage has displays of farm implements and other domestic appliances used in early 20th century Anglesey.

The former house is of a traditional type of cottage, found in Celtic zones of the British Isles which were the homes of 'poor labouring classes of rural areas'. Swtan is run by a group of volunteers and is an interesting attraction worth visiting.

It is only a few miles inland from here to another restoration scheme – the Llynon windmill at **Llanddeusant**. There is something calming about watching the arms of a windmill rotating round, in this case grinding wholemeal flour. You can also see the grindstones rotating in the mill and there is a shop on site selling lots of goods produced in Anglesey, including the flour.

A little to the north of Porth Swtan, or Church Bay, is a remarkable place; a small bay where a freak of nature has created a fascinating native reserve. The bay is Cemlyn Bay, to the west of Cemaes and the Wylfa nuclear power station.

However, halfway between this bay and Porth Swtan is an unusual rock arch projecting out into the sea. The rock arch is accessible at low tide. Perhaps the easiest way to find it is to park at Church Bay and walk up the coastal path towards **Carmel Head**. It is possible to get closer by car. A lane to Mynachdy farm has a nearby car-park with a much shorter walk to the coast, bringing you out close to the rock arch, known as Ynys Fydlyn.

Cemlyn Bay has a lane taking you to a small car-park adjacent to the beach. The main feature here is a bar made up of countless stones flung up by the sea, which runs right across the bay. The shingle bar has been here for some time, it is shown on the 1841 OS map. Beyond it is a good-sized lake of brackish water, well stocked with grey mullet. The marginal areas are the home to various wildfowl, including an impressive colony of 1,100 Sandwich terns. The area is a nature reserve owned by the National Trust and leased to the North Wales Wildlife Trust. On the west side of the bay are a group of ruined buildings of considerable age. There is an interpretation board on the reserve near to the car-park. You are requested to keep away from the reserve during the period of nesting, but the bar of shingle permits a good view of the reserve in any case. Look out for the sea cabbage which thrives amongst the stones.

The coastal lane from Cemlyn Bay continues on to the small and close-knit community of **Cemaes**, situated beside a sandy bay. The coastal path is particularly scenic in this area, although the power station mars the effect. Just off Carmel Head are a group of rocks known as The Skerries. It is a Nordic word, more commonly met within Scotland, where the name is frequently found, both on the west coast and right up to the Out Skerries in Shetland. The **Wylfa Nuclear Power Station** has a visitor centre.

A little further east is Amlwch and off the A5025, just out of Cemaes on the road to Amlwch, is a lane to **Llanbadrig**. The church is unusually dedicated to St Patrick and there is a traditional story that he was shipwrecked on Middle Mouse Island just off shore here and visible from the church. There is a car-park adjacent to the small church if you want to explore the area.

Although Cemaes had a small port and was a centre for shipbuilding, it was eclipsed by the port of **Amlwch**. Today the elongated port area is like a wide channel with steep walls, empty of water at low-tide. From the 1770s to 1815, however, Amlwch was a very busy place. It was where copper ore was shipped from the Parys and Mona Mines on nearby Parys Mountain.

Although the majority of the mine records do not survive, this was a huge deposit, worked by opencast, leaving an ugly scar on the landscape, which has never recovered despite the passage of nearly two centuries. Most of the area still does not support grass. It was very rich and Thomas Williams, the major shareholder, controlled the English copper market as a result (he was known as the Copper King). Even *HMS Victory* was sheathed around her hull with Anglesey copper. However, the profits were dulled by the huge amount of borrowings owed by the concern. Intriguingly, recent exploration work has proved that huge deposits of minerals remain, including gold.

The **old sail loft** at the quayside is now a small museum run by volunteers, with a tearoom and a display on the former copper industry. It is a far cry from the late 18th century when huge tonnages of ore left the port and large quantities of coal (any ore smelted here needed at least 3-4 tons of coal for every ton of ore). Moreover, a lot of the ore was very sulphurous, requiring roasting (again with coal) for months in order to drive it off. Amlwch had the mine brickworks which also needed coal. Additionally anything the mine needed – tools, gunpowder, timber, ropes, oil etc – had to be brought in by boat of one size or another.

Beyond Amlwch, at **Point Lynas**, the coastline turns south and its character begins to change too. Within 5 miles/8km is **Dulas Bay**, the first of several sandy bays to be

Above and below: Maritime Museum, Holyhead

Above: Breakwater Country Park, Holyhead

Below: Llynon Windmill, Llanddeusant

found. There are several, culminating with the broad expanse of Red Wharf Bay, or Treath-Coch. This is at Benllech, where the sea retreats a significant distance after high tide. Some of the beaches are nicely protected from the wind, such as the small beach at Moelfre.

Moelfre is a small community with a strong sense of identity and association with the sea. It is not just fishing or just being by the sea. For the hand of Providence has touched this area in a significant way on three occasions in relatively recent times. All connected with people on vessels, caught up in dramas beyond their own making, unexpected and profound.

In the case of the first, in 1859 and the third, in 1959, the events were 100 years apart to the day; the weather pattern identical, the manner in which the storm developed and the fate of the vessel identical; both just to the north-west of Moelfre on the same beach/rocks. Who says lightening doesn't strike twice.

The Royal Charter

The first event was the loss of **The Royal Charter** a luxury steam clipper with auxiliary sails on three masts. She weighed 2,719 tons and was en-route from Melbourne to Liverpool. She was a powerful vessel and had cut the journey time down to 60 days. On board were 324 passengers with a crew of 103. Only 39

survived, assisted by 28 villagers who brought them out of the water. There are several memorials of this. One is on the cliffs just beyond the headland at Moelfre and where the ship met her end. Another is at **Llanallgo Church**, just outside Moelfre, where 140 of those lost were laid to rest; another memorial is at the Sea Watch Centre, Moelfre. Others are where more of the dead were interred and there are a total of 388 of them, drowned or hurled by an uncompromising sea into the rocks upon which the ship met her fate and they met their maker. At nearby Penrhos Lligary are 45 interments.

The ship was one of 223 vessels which were lost on the night of 25-26 October, 1859. Over 800 people were lost in all. The other deceased passengers of The Royal Charter were buried at Penrhoslligwy, Llaneugrad, Llanwenllwyfo, Llanfairmathafarneithaf, Llanbedrgoch, Pentraeth, Llanddona, Amwlch and Llandudno (where some bodies were washed up). This detail is taken from the memorial in Llanallgo churchyard. The memorial was erected from subscriptions raised to pay for it. Charles Dickens (then a journalist on *The Times*) was instrumental in raising these subscriptions. By the memorial is one of the Royal Charter's anchors.

The vessel had taken refuge against a south easterly wind, which gained strength and turned to east-north-east, driving the vessel towards the coast. The wind speed increased to Force 12 and her anchors held until 1.30am when the port cable snapped, followed by the starboard cable an hour later. Thereafter, at the mercy of the sea, she swung to port and hit the rocks bow on. Interest in the wreck seems to have been less in the atrocious loss of life than in a small part of her cargo (by weight), for she was carrying bullion, gold dust and sovereigns valued at £322,440.00. However, many of her passengers were returning home having made a fortune in the gold fields. It was speculated that they could have accounted for a further £150,000.00 in gold sovereigns aboard the ship.

Divers soon recovered 90 per cent of the bullion, but how many of the passenger's sovereigns were recovered has remained an enigma. Does the sea hold a final secret under the surface of the waters near Moelfre's headland?

The latest memorial is at the Sea Watch Centre. Here two bronze panels face each other close to the Dick Evans statue. One panel portrays the ship breaking up on the rocks. The other shows one of the ship's crew, Joe Rodgers, who swam ashore with a rope attached. He climbed the rocks and the rope helped in the rescue of the 39 survivors.

The third event (the second follows!) concerned another vessel, this time a coaster in ballast. There was no intrigue this time, but there was a story; and it was about a successful lifeboat rescue. Now our lifeboat service is something dear to many of us but this story is the stuff of legend, not just borne out of affection.

The M.V. Hindlea

As befits a seafaring nation, the work of our lifeboat crews sits snugly against the breast of most of us. There can be little short of total admiration and respect for generations of men – many in a long line of family crewmen – who go to sea in times of dire need and risk.

On the centenary of the sinking of *The Royal Charter*, at a memorial service at Llanallgo Church, near Moelfre, where 140 victims of that vessel were laid to rest, few could have foreseen the events of the following day (26th October 1959). Moelfre lifeboat was being refitted at Beaumaris and a relief lifeboat had been allocated to Moelfre. It had just been brought from Pwllheli by Coxwain Richard Evans and his crew.

Events were about to unfold as the crew left the memorial service, which leave most of us in utter awe at the action of unassuming men, showing complete commitment, in the face of appalling seas and undeniable personal risk, placing all in the hands of Providence plus bravery and seamanship of the highest order.

Above: Llyn Alaw

Below: Swtan, Church Bay

Above: The shingle bar at Cemlyn Bay

Below: The lake at Cemlyn Bay nature reserve

This was the crew's destiny the following day. It was not even the full crew. With telephone lines down and firing a maroon impossible due to the hurricane winds, only five men were to be on board. One man, Hugh Jones, had never been on a lifeboat before, not even for an exercise.

Richard Evans had been alerted to the plight of the 506-tons/514tonnes *Hindlea*, caught in raging seas, whipped up by winds moving from south westerly to east northeast, which were strengthening and which were to record hurricane force that day. He realised that he could not reach his full crew and set off with the four crew members. He had realised that the conditions which beset *The Royal Charter* were repeating themselves as he headed for sea.

The *Hindlea*, just around the headland past Moelfre Island, was riding on her starboard anchor, but it was dragging towards the rocks on the shoreline. Approaching the *Hindlea*, the waves battered both ship and lifeboat as the sea boiled, the *Hindlea's* screws out of the water as often as they were in it.

For ninety minutes the skipper had hesitated and now Evans was only 200 yds/183m from rocks in worsened seas. The ship's anchor finally snapped and the skipper ordered the crew to abandon ship. Riding a beam-sea, with the side of the lifeboat broadside on to the sea, the lifeboat was caught by a wave which tipped it onto its beam ends, the mast under water. Evans managed to righten his boat and at last moved in.

Aligning his boat, the *E & M Robinson*, to the stern of the stricken ship, in 40 ft/12m waves and with winds exceeding 100 mph/160km, he saw his boat slammed against the ship's hull. The crew were on the poop deck on the stern and a crew member dropped onto the lifeboat. Undeterred, his boat still intact, he went around, measured his approach and ran in again.

In desperate conditions he aimed for the vessel ahead. As he pitched and rolled as close as he could, the ships screws rose above him. Going in once showed exemplary bravery, but he turned and approached a total of ten times in all. On the last approach a huge wave lifted up the lifeboat and dropped it on the *Hindlea's* deck, the final crewman clinging to the outside of the rail.

The mission seemed over, the next wave expected to tip them over and off the deck into the boiling white cauldron below. Yet the next wave lifted them even higher and they cleared the ship's rail. As the lifeboat pushed along the ship's side, two of the lifeboat men grabbed the remaining crewman as the lifeboat rushed past him. How they saw him in such waters was incredible, but they had him as they tumbled back onto their deck. Evan's rode the wave down to lower waters with one final task: to deliver his boat, crew and survivors to Moelfre, past jagged rocks lost from sight. He had only his memory and limited vision from reddened, salt-pained eyes to rely on, lashed as he was by a rope to his wheel.

His action that night earned him and his crew a **legendary place in maritime history** and the rare RNLI gold medal for bravery to himself. He was to repeat it again, one of only a few men to receive two gold medals. The late Henry Blogg of Cromer, is the only person to have received three.

The esteem and respect held locally for Richard Evans, BEM., may be measured today in the full-size bronze statue of him at a ship's wheel, looking towards the sea, in sight of the lifeboat station and situated adjacent to the Seawatch Centre. If you are down by the beach, look out for a salvaged anchor; it is off the *Hindlea*.

Longfellow wrote (in *The Galley of Count Arnaldos*):

'Woulds't thou' – so the helmsman answered –

'Learn the secret of the sea?

Only those who brave its dangers Comprehend its mystery'.

Maybe so, but here in a (relatively) quiet corner of Anglesey, we remember brave men with a sense of pride, trying to comprehend the events of that day, when the call of the *Hindlea* was answered.

In the morning, the ship lay on the rocks, broken in two, sharing the same fate as *The Royal Charter*.

At the time of the *Hindlea* incident, no doubt the crew would have liked a self-righting boat. In fact there was only one in service at the time and she had been introduced almost exactly one year before the rescue (21st October 1958 at Scarborough). The first one to be introduced in Wales (and only the 7th in Britain) went to Llandudno in 1964. Coincidentally, a boat of this class, the *Birds Eye*, has been preserved in the **Seawatch Centre** at Moelfre since 1991. The Centre is situated adjacent to the bronze statue to Dick Evans. If approached by road, follow the road through Moelfre along the seafront and when it turns left, keep going until you reach it on your right.

By comparison, the *Robinson* boat used in the *Hindlea* rescue and built in 1938 had 2 x 35bhp engines and cost £6,533.00. The Llandudno boat could draw 104hp, cost six times as much and was nearly 2 tons lighter at 12 tons 8cwt. Both had the coxwain's cockpit (where he manned the wheel) in the open. He was usually soaked through as soon as the boat hit the water on a slipway launch as at Moelfre. The cockpit on the *Birds Eye* was added in the 1980s. She was built in 1970 and went into service in July 1970 six months after Dick Evans retired. She was withdrawn in 1990, the year

Above: Cemaes

Below: Llanbadrig Church and Middle Mouse Island

Above: Amlwch Harbour

Below: Moelfre beach

Dick Evans died aged 86 years.

Dick's regular boat at Moelfre, the *Watkin Williams*, is preserved in Swansea. The *Hindlea* lifeboat, the *Edmund and Mary Robinson* also survives in private hands, having been sold in 2009. She has been much altered, however. At Whitby, you can go on a pleasure trip on the former RNLI's *Mary Ann Hepworth*. She is a sister boat to the *E & M Robinson*.

The loss and recovery of *HMS Thetis*

In 1936, the Admiralty ordered a new T-class of submarines from Cammell Laird's yard, Birkenhead. The third one, *HMS Thetis* headed for sea for the first time on the 1st June, 1939. Submerging in Liverpool Bay, she did not return to the surface. Four men got away, but 99 men died of carbon monoxide poisoning. Caught by a current, she drifted away from her dive position and was lost before she was found in the autumn in Liverpool Bay.

Having been found, the Admiralty dispatched a ship to the submarine. Wires were passed underneath her and *Thetis* was lifted off the bottom of the bay. Slung beneath the salvage vessel, she was carried 12 miles/ 19km to Anglesey and beached at **Treath Bychan**, the next bay to the east of Moelfre.

The cause of the accident was clear to see, a torpedo tube outer-door was open. Clearly the inner door had been opened and the sub's forward compartment flooded. She was beached some five months after the accident with the bodies still on board. Apparently, volunteers to recover the men were sought amongst the miners of South Wales; men who were known to be able to cope with the work of recovery.

The sub was refurbished and eventually sailed into the war as *HMS Thunderbolt*. She was later destroyed by depth charges from the Italian Navy in 1943. However, one reminder of her remains in the submarine service to this day. All the vessels are fitted with a safety device in the torpedo tube, known as a Thetis valve.

The dead were taken to Holyhead for burial and interred at the cemetery.

Ivor Wynne Jones in his seminal work *Shipwrecks of North Wales* records some 367 wrecks around the Anglesey coast. And there must be many more which are not recorded.

The coastal path from Moelfre to Dulas Bay starts from the Moelfre Beach and simply follows the coast, past the old lifeboat station and then the statue to Dick Evans at the Seawatch Centre just before the current lifeboat station is reached. It is a short distance from here to the headland, with **Moelfre Island** to your right, just off shore.

On the headland, immediately out to sea in front of you, is a plaque recording the bravery of the lifeboat crew involved in the *Hindlea* rescue. The ship was wrecked a short distance to your left and one wonders whether some steelwork on the rocks has anything to do with the wreck. It is about a half mile or so farther on to the *Royal Charter* memorial on the cliff above where this vessel was wrecked. It can clearly be seen from the headland.

The cliffs are not high and compose of a resistant thick bed of limestone with a rocky shelf below. The 40ft/12m waves which pushed the *Hindlea* onto the rocks would have cleared the top of these cliffs. It is these limestone beds which are responsible for the rare calcareous fenland nearby (see p48), now National Nature Reserves because of their importance and rarity.

Leaving Moelfre on the A5108, one reaches a roundabout after about a mile. Just over this, on the left in the small **Llanallgo Church**, with its *Royal Charter* memorial. A right turn at the roundabout leads to three closely situated archaeological sites, worth stopping to see.

After half a mile or so, on the right, is the Lligwy burial chamber, with a capstone weighing c. 25 tons. It is believed to date from c. 3000BC.

Some 350 yds/320m further on is a signpost to the left to **Din Lligwy**. This is a Romano – British village dating from the 3rd-4th century. However, also visible from the signpost, the width of a field away is **Capel Lligwy**, the remains of a medieval chapel, with enough remaining to give a good idea of how it would have looked.

Din Lligwy is across two fields, at the edge of a large wooded area. It is a fascinating place to visit. For one thing, the huge size of some of the stones used raises questions of logistics. There are several house sites here. Given that the roof of each building would be only a few feet from the ground, some of the walls must be fairly close to being intact. Most of the houses would have been rectangular with one circular. There is evidence of iron working and possibly iron smelting. There are good views from this area out into Dulas Bay to Ynys Dulas and its navigational tower. One is marked here on the 1841 OS map.

Adjacent to **Benllech**, within 3 miles/5km of Moelfre is **Red Wharf Bay**, a large expanse of sand where the sea recedes perhaps a mile or so at low tide. It is well known for its picturesque inn on the Benllech side of the bay. It is a popular place and many customers spill out onto the seating outside, and who blames them. There are caravan sites galore in this area – well perhaps a dozen or so, indicative of the long standing popularity of the bay.

Beyond here it is but a short distance to the headland of **Penmon**

Above: The statue of Richard Evans, B.E.M., Moelfre

Below: Moelfre Island

bove: Royal Charter Memorial, n the headland above the reck site

bove right: Llanallgo Church

ght: The Medieval church near n Lligwy, near Moelfre

Point and Puffin Island. The Point is reached by taking the road from Beaumaris past the castle (the B5109) and following the signs. Eventually you reach a kiosk where you have to pay a small toll to continue. It is, however, well worth continuing on to see Penmon Priory.

The main building here is part house, part church and part ruin. The ecclesiastical buildings are Norman but the dovecote east of the church is later, dating from c. 1600. Nearby is St Seiriol's well, which may account for the situation of the priory.

Continuing along the road, having paid the toll, the road ends at the Point with a dramatic view of the lighthouse, painted in broad bands of white and black and situated just off shore. There are a few cottages here, which enjoy the view to Puffin Island (formerly Priestholme).

At **Llangred**, near Beaumaris there is a car-park and a trail to nearby **Castell Aberlleiniog**, the only example on the island of a Norman **motte and bailey castle**. It dates from c. 1088 and the remains have recently been restored.

The main centre of population at this end of the island is **Beaumaris**. There are not many French names surviving in Wales, let along north-west Wales and it takes its name from the marsh which was drained by the castle fosse. The castle was never finished, having been started after The Statue of Ruddlan, which saw Wales ceded to Edward I. He built

Puffin Island

Previously known as Priestholme (Ynys Seiriol), it is understood to belong to the Williams – Bulkeley family of nearby Red Hill. It is closed to visitors unless permission has been granted. It extends to around 60 acres/24hec and is uninhabited.

There is a large population of sea birds including over 750 pairs of cormorant. Now that the rats have been destroyed, the puffins are making a comeback, having been virtually wiped out.

The island is now a Special Protected Area, because of its bird population, especially the cormorants.

In the 12th century there was a monastery here, part of the **Penmon Priory** complex nearby on Anglesey. Remains of this may be seen. St Seiriol is believed to be buried here.

There are cruises around the island from Beaumaris. Bookings are taken at Beaumaris pier, or ☎ 01248 810251 (Starida Sea Services). Grey seals may be seen on the rocks.

RSPB Cymru also runs a cruise around the island ☎ 02920 353008 for details. These also leave from the pier. Unfortunately, they are infrequent and may therefore not fit in with your travel plans. Advance booking is recommended.

the castles surviving in North Wales at Ruddlan, Conwy, Caernarfon, Harlech and Beaumaris (along with others).

The castle, a World Heritage Site, incorporates some sophisticated planning, which attacking soldiers would not have found appealing. Attacking forces faced 15 separate major obstacles and four successive lines of fortification. Nearly 3,000 men were employed in its construction. It was connected to the sea to enable ships to unload under the protection of the castle. It is the only North Wales castle where the moat survives complete with its water (at least partially). The castle dominates the small town and is a popular tourist attraction. Nearby are the town **Courthouse and Gaol**. The former retains its original furniture and is opposite the castle. It was built in 1614 and in use as a Court for well over 300 years, the oldest Courthouse in Wales in use at the time.

Beaumaris is fortunate that its Courthouse remains intact along with its jail in Steeple Lane, which still has cells, treadmill wheel and punishment cell. The wheel was not unusual in Britain's jails, but this is the only one to have survived. The jail was built in 1829.

The Bull's Head reflects a period when the town was of more importance. Ferryboats to Dublin went from here before moving to Holyhead. There were regular ferries to Liverpool (hence the Liverpool Arms – and there is another on Conwy's quayside too). It became the headquarters of General Mytton after he took the island for Cromwell in 1648. It was remodelled in 1766.

The main street, Castle Street, runs parallel to the sea front, separated from the town by a grassed recreational area, which adds to the town's charm.

It links with a much larger grassed area on the north side of the castle. Beaumaris has a pier where the ferry boats loaded and unloaded its passengers, to browse and promenade around the town, or wait while in transit to Dublin, Liverpool or the Welsh mainland at Penmaenmawr. Now it is much appreciated by anglers.

The Menai Strait separates Anglesey from the mainland. It is notorious for its current, which is particularly strong between the bridges at The Swellies. Although there are significant deposits of sand at either end of The Strait, the current sweeps away all signs of it along its length.

The road between Beaumaris and **Menai Bridge** holds little of interest for the visitors – ribbon development hiding views to the Strait. Prior to reaching Menai Bridge is Cadnant Inlet, where the old road descended to a bridge adjacent to the current highway. It was at the Inlet that Mytton's troops landed in 1648 during the Civil War.

HYDREF 28 1959 28 OCTOBER

ACHUBODD YR RNLB	THE RNLB
E a M ROBINSON	E and M ROBINSON RESCUED THE
GRIW Y LLONG HINDLEA	CREW OF THE M/V HINDLEA
DAN Y PENRHYN HWN.	OFF THIS HEADLAND.
COFIWN DDEWRDER	WE REMEMBER THE BRAVERY OF

COX. DICK EVANS

2ND COX MURLEY FRANCIS   MECHANIC EVAN OWENS
VOLUNTEER HUGH JONES   BOWMAN HUGH OWEN

Above: Memorial to the M.V. Hindlea rescue

Below: Moelfre Seawatch Centre & Royal Charter Memorial

Above: Din Lligwy round house

Below: Din Lligwy rectangular building

At the approach to Menai Bridge, take the road left immediately prior to the bridge approach. It leads down to the Strait at the foot of the bridge towers which dominate your view. It is most dramatic and worth the detour, especially if your camera is handy. For the best panoramic view of Menai Bridge, take the A4080 towards the Britannia Bridge. There is a long lay-by on your left; pull up here and marvel at the supreme achievement of Thomas Telford in 1826.

The Anglesey Interior

Compared with the dramatic coastline with its cliffs and sandy bays, the interior has nothing to match. It has long been noted for its good agricultural land, however, and was once regarded as the breadbasket of Wales. However, it has three important nature reserves, conveniently quite close to each other and other attractions. Mention has already been made of the Llanddeusant windmill (see p28).

Llangefni is the main community of the interior and its market day is on Thursdays. On the outskirts is **Oriel Ynys Mon**, which has displays of the island's heritage presented in an interesting manner. A look at the OS map indicates the high number of prehistoric burial mounds, standing stones which remind us of the wealth of evidence of the island's prehistoric past.

The Anglesey Fens

In the eastern interior of Anglesey, the underlying limestone contributes to the maintenance of the second most important calcareous fenland in Britain. It creates a habit for various species which are of national importance. There are three sites open to the public, all on National Nature Reserves and all three north or north-east of Llangefni. The Anglesey Fens are collectively part of a larger special area of Conservation extending to 1,154 acres/467ha.

Amongst an impressive collection of rare species of plants and invertebrates are fly orchid, marsh orchid, marsh helleborine and slender sedge. The fens are also the only location in north Wales for the southern damselfly. The rare marsh fritillary butterfly also flourishes here. The three National Nature Reserves enable the fens to be seen from footpaths and boardwalks. However, care is needed as fens are intrinsically, not for the unwary. Also, Welsh Mountain ponies graze the land (plus cattle) to keep the grass down and their natural curiosity should not be encouraged.

Cors Erddreiniog SSSI: 714 acre/289ha

Access to the site is down a track from Capel Coch, 4 miles/6km west of Benllech. This reserve involves more of a walk from Capel Coch.

Cors Goch SSSI: 133 acre/54ha

South-west of Benllech, go north

from Llanbedrgoch for about a mile and look for a narrow track on the left between housing. It is signposted for the reserve, which is reached at an obvious gate and interpretation board for the reserve. Climb over the stile and follow the track up onto heathland. Follow it around to the right and below you is the reserve with its cover of reeds.

Cors Bodeilio SSSI: 133 acre/54ha (about 10 per cent of this is the NNR)

The western end is a Common and open to public access, approached from Talwrn, north-west of Llangefni. Alternatively, if you are travelling along the A5025 from the Britannia Bridge (Junction 8 on the A55) in Pentraeth (5 miles/8km), turn left and then left again through the housing estate. After about 1.5 miles/2.5km from Pentraeth you descend from a ridge and the flat reed covered reserve is ahead of you. So is the entrance (where the road turns sharp left and the private road to 'Penrhyn' goes right). You can walk around the reserve perimeter for quite a distance on a flat, elevated board-walk. It has a few benches so that you can sit for a while.

There are adders on this site but you should be alright on the board-walk. The majority of this site is owned by the North Wales Wildlife Trust.

South-west of Amlwch is **Llyn Alaw**, a reservoir augmenting local water supplies. At the south-west end is a visitor centre open in the summer season and a car-park/picnic area. There is a further, much smaller reservoir (Cefni reservoir), just west of Llangefni with a picnic area at it northern end, near to Rhosmeirch village. The latter is only a couple of miles from Llanddeusant and the Llynon Windmill, which is in full working order grinding flour.

Close to junction 8 on the A55 is **Pili Palas Nature World**. Pili is Welsh for butterfly, but this is much more than a butterfly house. There are lots of birds and beasts at this all weather attraction, with plenty to occupy younger visitors. It is also open daily (except Dec 25/26) and worth remembering on both wet and wintry days.

In Conclusion

Anglesey has an interesting maritime past, a lovely coastline with a recently created coastal-footpath around the island, memorable views and lots of sandy beaches. It has much to offer the discerning tourist, families with young children, yachtsmen and women, wildlife lovers etc. It is the perfect compliment to the adjacent mountainous area of Snowdonia. An area long under-rated, it has much to offer; a lovely place for a short break or longer vacation.

Above: Red Wharf Bay

Below: Puffin Island

Above: Penmon Priory

Below: Beaumaris Court House

FACT FILE

ACCOMMODATION

There is a great range of accommodation available in Anglesey and throughout North Wales, everything from caravans and guest houses to luxury hotels. Many visitors will have booked their stay in advance, but for those who cannot, or are content to tour without prior booking, many Tourist Information Centres offer a bed booking service. This service is designed to give information on type, style and prices of accommodation and will recommend the most suitable for your requirements.

If you prefer to scout about for your own accommodation the Tourist Information Centres can generally supply a list of hotels, guest houses and self-catering accommodation that is available in the locality.

PLACES TO VISIT

Houses and Gardens

Generally open daily between April and September.

Parc Glynllifon
6 miles southwest of Caernarfon on A499
☎ 01286 830222
One of 3 Grade 1 listed gardens in Gwynedd
Gallery, workshops, craft shop and café.§

Penrhyn Castle (National Trust)
Bangor, A5, one mile east of Bangor
☎ 01248 353084
Magnificent neo-Norman hall. Railway and doll museum. Restaurant.
Open: daily except Tuesday, end-March to end-October. 11am-5pm.
Opening times vary.

Plas Newydd (National Trust)
Llanfair PG, Anglesey. 1 mile (1.6 km) south-west of Llanfair PG on A4080
☎ 01248 713673
On edge of Menai Straits, home of Marquess of Anglesey. Military Museum, restaurant.
Open: daily end-March to end-October except Thursday and Friday, 12noon–5pm.

Plas-yn-Rhiw
On Lleyn Peninsula south of Pwllheli, on the road to Aberdaron.
Open: April–October. Times vary.
Small seventeenth-century manor house in beautiful setting.
☎ 01758 780219

INFORMATION CENTRES – GANOLFAN CROESO CYMRU

Holyhead
Stena Line, Terminal 1, LL65 1DQ
☎ 01407 762622
e: Holyhead@nwtic.com

LlanfairPG
Station Site, LL61 5UJ
☎ 01248 713177
e: llanfairpwll@nwtic.com

Caernarfon
Oriel Pendeitsh, Castle St., LL55 1ES
☎ 01286 672232
e: Caernarfon.tic@gwynedd.gov.uk

MUSEUMS AND ART GALLERIES

Some museums are run by the local councils and are open all year round. Privately owned museums are generally open only during summer months. Most have gift shops and cafés.

Aviation Museum
Caernarfon Airport
☎ 01286 830800
Open: March to end-October, 9am-6pm

Gwynedd Museum & Art Gallery
Ffordd Gwynedd, Bangor
☎ 01248 353368
Open: Saturday, 10.30am-4.30pm;
Tuesday-Friday, 12.30-4.30pm

Holyhead Maritime Museum
Rhos-y-Gaer Avenue, Holyhead
☎ 01407 769745
Open: daily May–September except Mondays. Open Bank Holidays.

Museum of Childhood Memories
Water Street, Menai Bridge, Anglesey
Open: Easter–Oct Monday–Saturday, 10am–6pm, Sunday, 1–5pm.
Collection of everything to do with children over the last 150 years.

Oriel Ynys Mon
Rhosmeirch, Llangefni, Anglesey
☎ 01248 724444
Open: daily, 10.30am-5pm
History and Art Exhibitions.

**Segontium Roman Fort
and Museum** (National Trust)
1 mile (1.6 km) south of Caernarfon on A4085
Open: mid-March–mid-October, Monday–Saturday, 9.30am–6.30pm; Sunday, 2–6.30pm; Mid-October–mid-March, Monday–Saturday, 9.30am–4pm, Sunday, 2–4pm.

Archaeological finds
Seiont II Maritime Museum
Victoria Dock, Caernarfon
Open: daily Easter–September
Visit working steam boat.

RSPB
**Ellin's Tower RSPB Seabird Centre
South Stack, Anglesey**
Telescopes and remote-controlled cameras at Ellin's Tower Information Centre.
☎ 01407 764973
Open: daily, Easter – end Sept, 10am–5.30pm

Above: Beaumaris Castle

Below: Cors Bodeilio National Nature Reserve

Above: Cors Goch National Nature Reserve

Below: Oriel Ynys Mon, Llangefni

OTHER PLACES OF INTEREST

Heritage

Beaumaris Castle CADW
Beaumaris LL58 8AP
Dating from 1295 and very
impressive, if not actually completed.
☎ 01248 810361
Open : daily 9.30–5pm

Beaumaris Courthouse
Opposite castle entrance
☎ 01248 810921/811691
Oldest and most original courthouse
in Wales.
Open: daily except Fri, 10.30–5pm

Beaumaris Jail
Church Street, Beaumaris, Anglesey
Open: May-September, daily 11am–
6pm.
Grim but interesting reminder of
prison life in the past.
Open: daily except Fri, 10.30–5pm

Llynnon Windmill
Llanddeusant
☎ 01407 730407
Fully working windmill, shop selling
Anglesey produce including flour
from the mill
Open: daily 11am–5pm

Menai Bridge Experience
Menai Bridge LL59 5EA
☎ 01248 715046
Exhibition on the Britannia bridge
Open: Easter, Spring BH, July-Sept,
Sunday – Thurs, 10am–4pm

Sail Loft Visitor Centre
Amlwch Port LL68 9DB
☎ 01407 832255
Exhibition on local copper mining
and ship building
Open: Easter – end Sept, 10am–5pm

Seawatch Centre
Moelfre
☎ 01248 410277
Maritime history, preserved early self-
righting lifeboat
Open: Tues – Sat, 11am–5pm; Sun
1pm–5pm

South Stack Lighthouse
Holyhead
☎ 01407 763207/01248 724444
Open: daily 10.30–5pm

Swtan
Church Bay
☎ 01407 730186
Last thatched cottage on the island.
By the public carpark. Important
survivor of a Celtic farm cottage

Power Station
Wylfa Power Station
Cemaes Bay, Anglesey
☎ 01407 711400
Tours at 10.15am and 2pm Monday–
Friday, June–September. Observation
tower open daily.
Nuclear power station set on rugged
coast. Free

Zoos

Anglesey Sea Zoo
Brynsiecyn, Anglesey LL61 6TQ
☎ 01248 430411
Largest aquarium in Wales. Ideal
for children with unique collection.
Seafood centre and tea room.
Open: daily, Feb – Oct half term;
Weekends in winter

Pili Palas Nature World
Porthaethwy, Menai Bridge LL59 5RP
☎ 01248 712474
Butterflies from around the world
in natural habitat. Relax in exotic
surroundings, lots of other attractions
especially for children
Open: daily from 10am

OTHER ATTRACTIONS

Anglesey Model Village & gardens
Newborough LL61 6RS
☎ 01248 440477
Open: Easter – end Sept, 10.30am
– 5pm

Foel Farm Park
Brynsiencyn LL61 6TQ
☎ 01248 430646
Open: late Mar – end Oct, 10.30am–
5.30pm

RIDING/ADVENTURE

Isle of Anglesey Riding Centre
Dwyran LL61 6LQ
☎ 01248 430377
Open daily except Mon

Adventue Boat Rides
RibRide
Victoria Dock, Caernarfon
☎ 0791 4040001
One hour cruise along the coast of
Anglesey and Menai Strait

LEISURE

Ucheldre Centre
Millbank, Holyhead LL65 1TE
☎ 01407 763361
Arts centre (in former chapel) with
shop, restaurant with traditional
Welsh home cooking. Entry free
Open: daily, 10am – 5pm, (Sundays
2pm–5pm)

Oriel Ynys Mon
Rhosmeirch
Llangefni LL77 7TQ
☎ 01248 724444
Out of town art gallery, history gallery
and various exhibitions in a new
setting. Shop and café. By the golf
course
Open: daily, 10.30am–5pm

Beaumaris Leisure Centre
☎ 01248 811200

RAILWAYS

Main line operators have regular passenger services along the North Wales
coast and to Holyhead. There are stations at Holyhead (which meets the
ferries), Valley, Rhosneigr, Ty Croes, Bodorgan, LlanfairPG and Bangor on the
mainland.

Welsh Highland Railway
(Festiniog Rly Company)
Waunfawr, Caernarfon
The terminus of the railway below the
castle walls, trips into the mountains
of Snowdonia on restored narrow
guage line.
☎ 01286 677018

Above: Bardsey Mountain

Above: The former tower, Bardsey Abbey ruins

Opposite page: The former Bardsey Abbey screen, Llanengan Church, Abersoch. Note the integral Miserere seats

Bardsey Island/ Ynys Enlli

Bardsey lies just off the end of the Lleyn Peninsular in North Wales. It extends to 1.5 miles/2.4km in length and 0.5 mile/0.8km in width. Its area is 444 acres/180ha.

Its profile is dominated by **Bardsey Mountain** (Mynydd Enlli) in the north, which rises to 548ft/167m. However, much of the island is low lying and flat, supporting a farm with cattle and sheep. The herd is c.30 cattle and 400 sheep at the time of writing.

The island is owned by the Bardsey Island Trust who look after various buildings on the island, renting them as summer holiday lets. The island is a National Nature Reserve, Site of Special Scientific Interest, an Area of Outstanding Natural Beauty and part of the Pen Llyn Special Area of Conservation, and therefore has to be carefully managed in order to maintain its significance for wildlife. The RSPB took on the farming tenancy in 2008 and Steve and Joanna Porter are employed to run the farm and manage the land, living there with their family all year round as the only permanent residents. Joanna spins some of their wool production, makes baskets from the willow grown in the traditional withy beds and Steve also maintains a colony of bees, which he introduced prior to moving to the island in 2007. Bardsey honey has a distinctive taste and sells quickly. The island also has its own species of apple. The population was 124 in 1901.

Much of the housing on the island was built by Lord Newbrough in the 1870s, although Carreg Bach, south of the chapel, is older. Ruins of the thirteenth century **Augustinian Abbey** survive. The abbey was closed in 1537 upon dissolution of the monasteries under Henry VIII. Although it is thought that the island has been used as a religious centre for much longer than the abbey, there are no significant remains.

Equally there remains a tradition that 20,000 saints are buried on the island. One wonders if this was meant in a spiritual, rather than a physical sense, although many remains have been found. Parts of the structure of the abbey (stone, timber etc) were incorporated in Llanengan Church – from where, incidentally, there is a good view of the island.

The tower here was built apparently in 1534 and if this is correct the removal of furnishings to Llanengan – the screen with its miserere stalls and the bell– in 1537 would seem to fit in nicely with the Llanengan rebuilding programme.

Llanengan Church has two screens, the left hand one appears to be purpose made for the church. The other is definitely '2nd-hand' as an empty mortice joint shows at the inner end. The 12 miserere stalls (low level seats) are attached to the altar-side of the screen. The church has three bells. Two are dated and 17th century. The other is undated and could be the Bardsey Abbey church bell. By the font is an ancient chest where donations from pilgrims bound for Bardsey were kept. The church is kept locked and the key kept at the nearby inn.

It is believed that the abbey was founded as early as 516 AD by St. Cadfan, after his arrival from Brittany. If so, it would have been one of the earliest foundations in Britain. Following the destruction of the monastery at Bangor–is-y-Coed after the Battle of Chester in c. 603, the monks moved to Bardsey, regarding it as a safer place to live.

Yet one cannot ignore the importance of Bardsey in a past era when much significance was placed on the value of making a pilgrimage. Three visits to the island was the equivalent of one to Rome. Old trackways can be traced along which many people made the journey, including the one from Caernarfon, past the venerable and fascinating church dedicated to St. Bueno at Clynnog Fawr, although it is of Tudor date.

There was, however, an earlier foundation at Clynnog Fawr. The church is believed to be the burial place of St. Bueno, who is supposed to have brought St. Winifred back to life at Holywell. The church has

an ancient chest in which offerings, made by pilgrims on their way to Bardsey, were kept. In fact the road from Llanaelhaern, just south of Clynnog Fawr, to Nefyn is known as the Saints Road to Bardsey. The road continues via Tudweiliog to Aberdaron where the little church on the edge of the beach, dedicated to St. Mary, was used to pray for a safe journey to the island.

The island also featured in an abortive attempt over a century later, in 1649, to seize the island for the Royalist cause. A party of eight, sailing from Ireland, arrived three days after some 30 soldiers landed to intercept them. All were captured and dispatched to Caernarfon Castle. The captain of their boat escaped back to Ireland and from the hands of Parliamentary justice.

The island has its own Bird Observatory, established in 1953 where one can also stay during the summer months. The island is on a migration route for many thousands of birds. There are some 40 different species nesting on the island, including a resident population of over 15,000 pairs of Manx shearwaters, which return to roost after dark. They will nest in both old rabbit burrows and make their own burrows in the old field banks or cloddiau. It is also a significant location for the Red legged Chough, which can often be seen feeding on the maritime grassland or doing acrobatics in the air above the mountain.

In addition to the **Bardsey apple**, there are several other rare plants including Rock Sea Lavender and two heathland lichens. There are over 350 species of lichens in total. An on-going count of moths has found 143 species in 2008. Around the coast may be seen inquisitive seals, now into their hundreds, plus porpoises and dolphins. You will most likely see the seals as you cross over to the small slipway on the east coast near to the narrow neck of land connecting the low part of the island to the flanks of Mynydd Enlli. The narrow stretch of water between the mainland and the island carries a strong current and the crossings are very much subject to weather conditions.

Bardsey has a distinctive **lighthouse**, with a range of 17 miles/27km. If you wonder why it is different, it is because it is square in cross section and the only one like this maintained by Trinity House. It has red and white banding and is just short of 100ft/35m tall. It was built in 1821 and still is an important navigational aid for local coastal traffic and vessels heading for Liverpool, Dublin etc.

Notice the railings at the top; these are original and survived the replacement of the initial lantern in 1856.

There is a **craft shop** on the island, open throughout the visitor season. It stocks Joanna's willow baskets, wool rugs, felted crafts, spun and knitted wool items, Steve's honey, Rachel Porter's handmade jewellery and Ben Porter's photographic cards.

FACT FILE

Bardsey Island Trust
Plas Glyn-y-Weddw
Llanbedrog
Pwllheli, Gwynedd
LL53 7TT
☎ 08458 11 22 33
The Trust welcomes new members

Bardsey Bird and Field
Observatory (www.bbfo.org)
Alicia Normand
Postal Address: 46 Maudlin Drive,
Teignmouth, Devon, TQ14 8SB
☎ 01626 773908

DAY TRIPS
Bardsey Boat Trips
☎ 07971 769895
www.bardseyboattrips.com
This ferry is based on the island in the summer. Sails from Porth Meudwy, near Aberdaron

Bardsey Island Ferry
☎ 08458 113655/07836 293146
www.enllicharter.co.uk
Sails from Pwllheli and Porth Meudwy
Sailings subject to weather conditions

ACCOMMODATION
The Bardsey Island Trust has seven self-catering houses on the island. These are two detached and three semi-detached houses, a cottage and a converted stable.
Details from the Trust (see above) and see the observatory website above.

Above: The lighthouse is the only square one maintained by Trinity House

Above: Baby seal and mother, Bardsey. They are best seen near the jetty

Index